D1168466

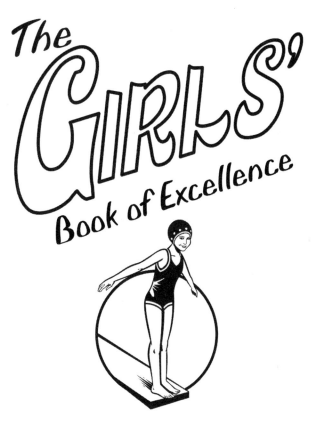

The GIRLS' Book of Excellence

Book of Excellence

EVEN MORE WAYS TO BE THE
BEST AT EVERYTHING

Written by Sally Norton
Illustrated by Katy Jackson
Edited by Philippa Wingate
Designed by Zoe Quayle

The GIRLS'
Book of Excellence

EVEN MORE WAYS TO BE THE
BEST AT EVERYTHING

SCHOLASTIC INC.

New York   Toronto   London   Auckland   Sydney
Mexico City   New Delhi   Hong Kong   Buenos Aires

For the delightful Kate Jeffrie

No part of this publication may be reproduced, stored in a retrieval system, or transmitted in any form or by any means, electronic, mechanical, photocopying, recording, or otherwise, without written permission of the publisher. For information regarding permission, write to Michael O'Mara Books Limited, 9 Lion Yard, Tremadoc Road, London SW4 7NQ, United Kingdom.

Library of Congress Cataloging-in-Publication data available.

ISBN-13: 978-0-545-13409-5
ISBN-10: 0-545-13409-9

First published in Great Britain in 2008 by Buster Books, an imprint of Michael O'Mara Books Limited, 9 Lion Yard, Tremadoc Road, London SW4 7NQ, United Kingdom.
www.mombooks.com/busterbooks

Text and illustrations copyright © 2008 Buster Books

Cover design by Angie Allison
(from an original design by www.blacksheep-uk.com)
Cover illustration by Paul Moran

12 11 10 9 8 7 6 5 4 3 2 1   9 10 11 12 13 14/0

Printed in the U.S.A.
First American edition, August 2009

NOTE TO READERS

CONTENTS

HOW TO BE THE BEST CHEERLEADER

Experienced cheerleaders put on amazing shows that include cartwheels, handsprings, and complicated jumps. If you can master the seven basic cheerleading moves described here, you can put them together in a pom-pom-tastic routine.

Practice to some loud, funky music with a great beat.

The High V: Stretch both arms up and out in a V-shape above your head. At the same time, jump your feet out to the sides. Hold for a count of three seconds, then shake your pom-poms. Finally, drop your arms back down to your sides.

The L Motion: Jump your feet together. Raise your left arm straight above your head and your right arm out to the side, so your arms form an L-shape. Hold for three seconds, then shake your pom-poms. Then reverse this move, so your right arm is in the air and your left arm is out to the side, and shake. Drop your arms back down to your sides.

The K Motion: With your feet together, raise your left arm up and out into the high V-shape. Move your right arm across your body so your right hand is level with your left hip. Hold for three seconds, then shake your pom-poms. Now reverse so your right arm is in the air and your left arm crosses your body.

Buckets: Jump your feet apart and bring your arms straight out in front of you with your fists facing down as though you're holding the handle of a bucket in each hand. Hold for three seconds, then shake your pom-poms.

The Banana: Jump your feet together. Arch backward and reach your arms up and behind you. Hold for three seconds, then shake. Straighten up and drop your arms to your sides.

The Touchdown: Jump your feet out to the sides. Lift both arms straight up above your head, palms facing each other. Hold for a count of three seconds. (This is the move cheerleaders use at football games when their team scores.)

The Knee Drop: Jump down into this final position with your right knee bent in front of you and your left knee on the floor as shown below. Hold your arms out in a high V-shape above your head and give those pom-poms one final shake while you shout out your favorite cheer.

TEAM TIME

Cheerleading is a team sport, so grab a group of friends and practice a routine that goes through all the basic moves one after another, in the order shown on pages 8 and 9.

Ask someone to count out 1-2-3-4, 1-2-3-4, throughout the routine to make sure you all keep in time with one another.

DRESS RIGHT

Your squad needs to look like a team, so it is important to match your outfits. Matching skirts or shorts with a T-shirt of your chosen color is a good choice. Get your teammates to tie their hair back into high ponytails and secure with ribbons in your team colors. Remember to always wear a big smile, even if your team is losing!

ADD A CHEER

Here are some cheers to try, or feel free to make up your own.

Two, four, six, eight.
Who do we appreciate?
Not the king, not the queen,
But our favorite football team!

Pom-poms up,
Pom-poms down,
We know our team's
The best in town.

We're the best,
We beat the rest.

HOW TO MAKE YOUR OWN POM-POMS

Cheerleaders hold a pom-pom in each hand. A pom-pom is a shaggy ball of plastic strips attached to a handle. You can buy these in a store or you can make your own with recycled plastic bags from the supermarket. Try to match the bags to your team colors.

You Will Need:

- six or ten bags per pom-pom, depending on how big you want them to be
- a ruler
- a felt-tip pen
- scissors
- masking tape or strong rubber bands

WHAT YOU DO

1. Smooth each bag out flat on the floor. Get a ruler and a pen. Measure 12 inches up from the base of the bag and draw a line.

2. Cut along the line, removing the top of the bag along with the handles.

3. Starting at the open end, cut about 8 inches down the depth of the bag, stopping 4 inches from the bottom. Repeat this across the whole width of the bag to form strips that are each about 1 inch wide.

4. Repeat the process with all your bags.

5. Gather the prepared bags, holding them at the uncut bases. To make a handle for your pom-pom, scrunch the bases together and secure by wrapping a long strip of masking tape around them or by using a strong rubber band. Finally, rub the finished pom-poms between your hands to fluff them up.

HOW TO MAKE ICE CREAM IN A PLASTIC BAG

You don't need an ice cream maker to make this delicious treat!

You Will Need:

- 1 gallon-size reclosable plastic bag
- ice cubes
- 6 tablespoons rock salt
- 1/2 cup cold milk
- 1/4 teaspoon vanilla extract

- 1 tablespoon sugar
- 1 pint-size reclosable plastic bag
- gloves (to keep your hands warm when handling the ice)

WHAT YOU DO

1. Fill the large plastic bag halfway with ice and add the rock salt.

2. Pour the milk, vanilla, and sugar into the small plastic bag and seal it tightly. Be sure to squeeze out any extra air.

3. Place the small bag inside the large one and seal tightly. Be sure to squeeze out any extra air.

4. Shake vigorously for five to ten minutes.

5. Take the small bag out of the large bag and wipe off the small bag to keep the salt out of your ice cream. Open the bag and enjoy!

HOW TO INTERPRET YOUR DOODLES

The doodles you draw when you're daydreaming may be an excellent way to discover what sort of person you really are inside. Next time you realize you have been off in a world of your own, covering a page in doodles, take a look at what you have drawn and find out what it all may mean below.

Geometric Shapes
You're a really organized person and the one people turn to when they want to get things done.

Flowers and Curves
You're friendly and understanding, and everyone loves you.

A House
You're a homebody who loves to feel safe and secure. You have everything you want right on your own doorstep.

Arrows

You've got big plans for your life and you're determined to reach your goals.

Hearts

You're romantic and emotional. You probably send lots of cards on Valentine's Day and get lots in return.

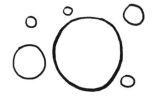

Circles

You enjoy being alone. The trouble is, everyone loves being around you, so you don't often get the chance.

Triangles

You get bored doing the same things every day, and you love change and a challenge.

Birds

You're a free spirit who just wants to fly away from it all.

HOW TO MAKE A CLOTHESPIN CHRISTMAS ANGEL

This clothespin angel doll is easy to make, and it will look great decorating a branch on your family's Christmas tree.

You Will Need:

- a round-headed wooden clothespin
- a felt-tip pen
- a pipe cleaner
- some cotton fabric
- scissors
- fabric glue
- a round paper doily
- cardboard
- glitter and sequins
- white, yellow, or brown yarn
- a ribbon

WHAT YOU DO

1. Draw your angel's eyes, and mouth on the clothespin with a felt-tip pen.

2. Wind a pipe cleaner around the "neck" of the clothespin to make two arms. Bend at each elbow.

3. Trim a piece of cotton fabric into a rectangle about 3 inches by 2 inches. Squirt some fabric glue along one edge and wrap the fabric around the angel's body just below the arms to form a tube. Use some more glue to stick it in place at the back.

4. Make a cut in the doily from the edge to the center. Cut a small circle at the center about the width of your clothespin. Wrap the doily skirt around the angel and stick in place with fabric glue.

5. Draw the shape of a pair of wings on cardboard and cut the wings out. Decorate with glitter and glue the wings to the back of your angel.

6. Cut five equal lengths of yarn and glue them on the angel's head to form her hair.

7. Add glitter and sequins to give your angel some sparkle.

8. Finally, cut a length of pretty ribbon and tie it around the angel's neck. Tie the two ends of the ribbon in a knot to form a hanging loop.

HOW TO SET UP A NAIL SALON

Why not set up a nail salon in your bedroom? Be sure to ask an adult first, then invite your friends over and impress them with your professional manicure skills.

TOP TRICKS AT YOUR FINGERTIPS

- File nails into a slightly squared oval. The "squoval" is the most flattering shape for all nails.

- Don't file too deeply into the sides of nails as you may break them.

- Keep an old pair of pantyhose in your manicure kit. Once you've finished filing a nail, make sure the tip is ultrasmooth by running it over the pantyhose. It shouldn't snag.

- Apply nail polish to a nail in three broad strokes: one down the side, one down the middle, and one down the other side. If you're using a dark color, two thin coats are better than one thick one.

- Don't use just the tip of the brush to apply polish or you'll apply too much and encourage air bubbles. The bristles should be splayed out horizontally against the nail. This means you'll get thinner, more even layers for a more professional finish.

- Dry wet nail polish in an instant by plunging your hands into a bowl of ice-cold water.

A QUICK FIX

A good manicurist always has neat nails herself, so make sure you take care of your own hands. If you want a manicured look but don't have time to polish your nails, try pouring a few drops of olive oil onto a clean, soft cloth and buffing them quickly.

If you've got an extra minute to spare, sweep the tip of a white nail pencil under the top edges of your nails for an instant French manicure look.

HOW TO MAKE A WALNUT-SHELL BOAT

If you crack a walnut really carefully, the shell will break into two perfect halves. In two minutes, you can transform them into boats that will float beautifully on water.

Cut a rectangle out of paper to create the sail. You can decorate it if you like. Then thread a toothpick through the paper to form a mast.

Push a small lump of modeling clay into the middle of the walnut half. Push one end of the toothpick into the modeling clay.

Grab a friend and head off to the nearest stream. Launch your boat and see which one sails into the sunset the fastest.

HOW TO DEAL WITH PIMPLES

As a general rule, pimples are best left alone. However, if you can't resist trying to treat them, remember that different pimples need different treatments. Always wash your hands before attempting any treatment.

RED PIMPLE

Never try to squeeze a pimple that's just a lump without a "head" on it. If you do, you'll just push the infection deeper and risk scarring your skin.

In the morning, hold an ice cube over the pimple for a few seconds to reduce the swelling and shrink the pimple.

Dab the pimple with antiseptic lotion or a little tea-tree oil at night. The pimple will soon start to clear.

YELLOW PIMPLE

If the pimple has come to a head and has a yellow top on it, you can try working on it very gently.

Make a cup of warm chamomile tea and dip a cotton ball in it. Then place the cotton ball on the pimple and hold it there for a minute.

Repeat this several times. Softening the skin like this will help to prevent any bruising and scarring when you start to tackle the pimple.

With a tissue covering your fingertips, gently apply a LITTLE pressure all around the spot until it deflates. Never use dirty fingers to touch a pimple as it could become infected and will look worse and last longer.

If the pimple doesn't pop right away when you apply gentle pressure, stop and try again another day.

Important: Never squeeze a pimple until it bleeds; this can scar your skin. Never cover a squeezed pimple with makeup until it's completely dried out.

HOW TO RECOGNIZE YOUR BIRTHSTONE

Gemstones are minerals or rocks that can be cut, polished, and used in beautiful jewelry. Some gemstones are linked to a particular month of the year and are known as birthstones. They make a special birthday gift, and some people say it's really lucky to wear your own birthstone.

Month	Birthstone	Color of Stone
JANUARY	garnet	dark red
FEBRUARY	amethyst	purple
MARCH	aquamarine	pale blue
APRIL	diamond	white
MAY	emerald	green
JUNE	moonstone (or pearl)	cream

Find out which is your birthstone in the chart below.

If you're not lucky enough to own your own birthstone (unfortunately, lots of them are very expensive), you can always paint a stone the correct color (see below).

Alternatively, try wearing an item of clothing that's the color of your birthstone.

Month	Birthstone	Color of Stone
JULY	ruby	red
AUGUST	peridot	pale green
SEPTEMBER	sapphire	deep blue
OCTOBER	pink tourmaline (or opal)	pink
NOVEMBER	yellow topaz	yellow
DECEMBER	turquoise (or blue topaz)	sky blue

HOW TO TRAIN YOUR BRAIN

You might not be the best at math or know all the capital cities of the world, but perhaps you're the most creative person in your family or school. Try this test to find out.

THE PAPER CLIP CHALLENGE

You can use paper clips to do much more than just clipping pieces of paper together. Spend two minutes writing down as many uses for paper clips as you can. Be as creative, daring, and silly as you like.

Once the two minutes are up, count up your ideas.

Four is the average number of uses people come up with.
Eight uses is high.
Twelve uses is rare.
Only one person in a thousand thinks of **sixteen** uses.

Get your friends and family to try to see who's the most creative.

GETTING STARTED

Here are some ideas to get you going. You could use paper clips . . .

. . . as bookmarks.

. . . to scatter on the beach in the hundreds and drive people using metal detectors crazy.

. . . as a prize in the world's worst raffle.

. . . as fishhooks.

. . . joined together to make a necklace.

. . . as a tiny pair of skis for a pet parakeet.

. . . to hold up a fallen hem on your skirt.

. . . to unclog a blocked pencil sharpener.

. . . for painting tiny dots on a picture.

. . . as the anchor of a walnut-shell boat (see page 19).

. . . as a jungle gym for fleas.

. . . as clothes hangers for dolls.

HOW TO GET GUM OUT OF YOUR HAIR

GUM, GOING, GONE

Hold an ice cube on the affected hair. This will make the chewing gum become really hard and cold. When it does, crack it with your fingers and pick off the bits.

Rub any stray remaining bits of gum with peanut butter. This may sound really strange, but peanut butter has a magical effect on chewing gum. Massage it in thoroughly.

Comb out the peanut butter with a fine-toothed comb.

Shampoo and condition your hair.

Finally, enjoy some creamy peanut butter as a reward for your hard work!

Warning: Don't eat or touch peanut butter if you have a nut allergy.

HOW TO MAKE A POTATO CHIP BAG BROOCH

You can make a fun, quirky brooch to wear or to pin to your backpack. Here's how:

You Will Need:

- a small bag of potato chips
- paper towels
- a baking sheet
- oven mitts
- a wooden spoon
- masking tape
- a safety pin

WHAT YOU DO

1. First, ask an adult for help and supervision. Turn the oven to its hottest setting.

2. Carefully open the bag of chips (try not to tear it!) and eat the contents.

3. Shake out any crumbs and wipe the inside of the bag clean with a paper towel.

4. Place the bag on a baking sheet and flatten it out as much as you can.

5. Place the sheet in the oven for around ten minutes. Check the bag every couple of minutes to make sure it doesn't burn. It should begin to shrink!

6. When the bag has shrunk to about two-thirds of its original size and is about 2 inches wide, take the sheet out of the oven using the oven mitts.

7. Using the back of a wooden spoon, quickly flatten out any kinks or curls in the bag. Then leave the bag to cool for five minutes.

8. Once the bag is completely cool, pick it up. It will now be much harder and thicker than a normal potato chip bag.

9. Tape a safety pin to the back of the bag.

10. Pin to your lapel or backpack. Stand back and wait for compliments!

HOW TO PLAY SEVENS

Sevens is a great ball game that you can play by yourself or with friends. The moves you have to make get harder the further you progress, so see how long you can keep going.

HOW TO PLAY

Find a tennis ball and a flat wall that is outdoors. Stand about 6 feet from the wall and follow this routine:

- Throw the ball at the wall and catch it.

- Throw the ball at the wall, let it bounce, then catch it.

- Throw the ball at the wall, swat it back at the wall with the palm of your hand, then catch it.

- Throw the ball at the wall, swat it back at the wall, let it bounce once, and catch it.

- Throw the ball at the wall, let it bounce once, bounce it again with the palm of your hand, and catch it.

- Throw the ball at the wall, swat it back at the wall, let it bounce once, bounce it again with your hand, and catch it.

- Throw the ball at the wall, swat it back at the wall, let it bounce, bounce it again, swat it back at the wall, and catch it.

MAKE IT HARDER

Add one of the following variations each time you go through the whole routine.

- Clap your hands each time you throw the ball.

- Clap your hands twice after throwing the ball.

- Spin around each time you throw the ball.

- Go through each stage using only your right hand.

- Repeat each stage using just your left hand.

- Start each stage by throwing the ball under your right leg.

- Now try each stage throwing the ball under your left leg.

If all that is just too easy, you can combine as many of your own variations as you like. Why not challenge a friend to a Sevens championship match?

HOW TO LOOK BEAUTIFUL TOMORROW

You can look even more fabulous in just one night!

Get Prettier Feet. There's no need to scrub away at dry heels and hard skin for hours. Simply slather on lots of thick body lotion, pull on some cotton socks, and head to bed. You'll wake up to much softer feet.

Get Smoother Lips. Slick chapped lips with petroleum jelly before bed. In the morning, rub gently with a clean, damp washcloth to remove any flakes of dead skin.

Get Softer Hands. Apply a dollop of hand cream right before bed. It will seal in extra moisture and work wonders on hands and nails while you're dreaming.

Get Shinier Hair. For the glossiest locks ever, just smooth lots of thick conditioner onto freshly shampooed hair before bedtime. Protect your pillow by covering it with an old towel. Rinse and style your hair in the morning.

Get Clearer Skin. Don't worry about that pimple ruining your day. Just dot on some diluted tea-tree oil before bed. It's the best pimple buster known to humankind.

HOW TO MAKE A HEN EGG COZY

If you can stitch two pieces of fabric together, you can make this gorgeous hen cozy for your boiled egg.

You Will Need:

- tracing paper
- a felt-tip pen
- straight pins
- brown felt for the body of the hen
- felt in a contrasting color for the wings and eyes of the hen
- scissors
- a large darning needle
- two lengths of embroidery thread (choose a color that contrasts with the felt)
- fabric glue

WHAT YOU DO

1. Place the tracing paper over the top of the pattern opposite and draw over the outline of the wing and the outline of the

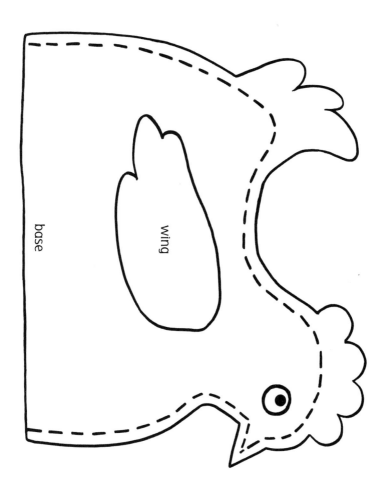

base

wing

body with a felt-tip pen. Then repeat so you have two sets of matching pieces (two bodies and two wings).

2. Cut out all the patterns from the tracing paper.

3. Pin the paper patterns to the felt and cut out the pieces.

4. Cut small circles of felt to create the hen's eyes.

5. Thread a needle and make a knot near the end of the thread. Join the two body shapes together using a simple running stitch around the edges. Working from right to left if you're right-handed (and from left to right if you're left-handed), push the needle in and out through both layers of the felt.

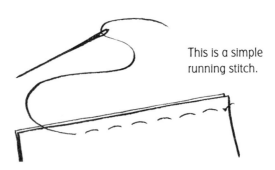

This is a simple running stitch.

6. You need to leave the base of the hen open. So when you get to the end, secure the last stitch that's closest to you by going back to the end of the last stitch that's closest to you and bringing the needle through the stitch again. Repeat. Snip off the remaining thread.

7. Use the glue to stick on the wings and eye shapes.

8. Place your hen cozy over an egg sitting in an egg cup. It will look so cute that you will be asked to make one for each member of your family. Soon your breakfast table will look like a hen coop.

HOW TO DRY FLOWERS

Dry the flowers and herbs you pick in the summer and you'll have a bedroom full of blooms all year round.

1. First, pick your flowers. Try to choose perfect plants with long stems. Roses and lavender work well.

2. Snip the stems neatly and pick off any leaves from the lower half of the stems.

3. Gather the flowers into small bunches, fastening them together with a rubber band.

4. Open each bunch into a fan shape so the air can get to every bloom.

5. Hang the flowers upside down in a dark, dry place for two or three weeks.

Display your dry flowers in a pretty vase or container. Do not add water.

A bunch of dried flowers makes a perfect gift for Mother's Day.

HOW TO CLEAN YOUR ROOM IN FIFTEEN MINUTES

Your bedroom might look as though a tornado just struck, but you can make it presentable in only fifteen minutes. When you see what you can achieve in just a quarter of an hour, you might even resolve to get really organized.

BEFORE YOU START

Put on some of your favorite music. If it has a great beat and you can sing along to it, the job will seem much more fun.

Grab a few trash bags, a tray, and a couple of empty boxes. You'll also need a damp cloth and a vacuum cleaner. Pull back the curtains and roll up the blinds. Open the windows to let some fresh air in while you clean.

HERE WE GO

Why not get someone to time you?

Fifteen Minutes to Go. Gather up all the stray clothes from around the room and dump them on the bed. Sort through them, putting dirty clothes into a laundry bag for washing, and remove the bag from the room. Put away the rest of your clothes in your closet and drawers, making sure they're properly shut afterward.

Twelve Minutes to Go. Gather items that don't belong in your room (like dirty dishes and things you have borrowed from your mom) and put them on a tray. Put the tray outside your bedroom door to be dealt with later.

Eleven Minutes to Go. Gather up everything that can be thrown away from the floor and from all visible surfaces. Dump it all in a trash bag (you can sort out items for recycling later on). Remove the bag from the room.

Nine Minutes to Go. Spend one minute gathering all stray DVDs, CDs, games, and stuffed animals together and putting them back where they belong. Do the most you can in the time.

Eight Minutes to Go. Spend one minute putting away books and shuffling papers into neat piles. Again, do as much as you can in the time.

Seven Minutes to Go. There's no time for thorough filing or sorting today. Gather together all remaining stray items (like photographs, magazines, and odd socks) that are lying around and dump them into an empty box — it's better than stuffing them all under the bed. Place the box in the corner of the room or under a table out of sight. Once everything is all together, you may feel inspired to tackle it.

Five Minutes to Go. Get a damp cloth and wipe any dusty surfaces.

Three Minutes to Go. Make your bed, taking care to straighten out the bedspread and plump up the pillows.

Two Minutes to Go. Vacuum the floor. Do the main part of the floor first, finishing with the corners and edges of the room if you have time.

Finished. Well done! You did a great job. Now how about the living room?

HOW TO HAVE THE SHINIEST SHOES EVER

A mirrorlike sheen on your leather shoes takes a little know-how and a lot of elbow grease, but it's worth it. Always place old newspaper over your work space before you begin. You should also wear old clothes because shoe polish will stain fabric.

1. Take out any laces and undo any straps.

2. Wipe off all dirt from the surface of your shoes with a damp cloth.

3. Remove any ingrained dirt or stains with saddle soap, which you can find at the supermarket. Rub a little bit of saddle soap into the shoe with a damp cloth. Then keep rubbing until the leather looks really clean.

4. Buff your shoes with a clean, dry cloth.

5. Use an old cotton T-shirt to apply some shoe polish. Unlike a brush, a T-shirt won't scratch the leather. Dab a small amount of polish onto the T-shirt, and rub it into the leather in small circles. Keep going until you see a shine start to appear. Continue over the whole shoe.

6. Leave your shoes on a piece of newspaper while the polish dries completely.

7. Grab a clean cotton cloth and buff the leather to a final shine.

Voilà! You now have beautiful shiny shoes.

HOW TO PLAY CLOCK SOLITAIRE

Here is a game of Solitaire played in a clock pattern. It's a perfect way to spend a rainy afternoon.

HOW TO PLAY

Deal twelve cards facedown in a pattern like the numbers on a clock face. Put another card in the center of your "clock." Repeat this until you have four cards in each pile.

Turn over the top card on the center pile. This card directs you to one of the piles on the clock face. Aces go at one o'clock, twos at two o'clock, all the way around to the jacks at eleven o'clock and queens at twelve o'clock. Place your card faceup under the pile or beside it, then turn over the top card of this pile to find out where to go next.

Whenever you turn over a king, you must place it in the center of the clock and take a card from the center pile to start again.

The goal is to turn over the cards in all twelve piles. Once you have revealed all four kings, though, the game is over.

HOW TO EAT A GOLDFISH

Don't panic! You don't really have to eat a goldfish. This is a great trick and is bound to cause quite a stir whenever you perform it. All you need is a goldfish bowl filled with water containing a thin slice of carrot cut into the shape of a goldfish. (Ask an adult to help you cut the piece of carrot.)

WHAT YOU DO

1. Stand between your friend and the bowl. Discreetly turn away from him or her and swirl the water in the bowl with your fingers. This will make the carrot "goldfish" appear to swim.

2. Turn back and announce that you're feeling hungry. Your friend may suggest a cookie or a piece of fruit. Refuse politely, telling him or her that you have a perfect high-protein snack in mind.

3. Plunge your hand into the bowl and pull out the "fish." Bounce it around in your palm a bit to make it look as though it's flapping around.

4. Pop the carrot into your mouth, crunch it, and swallow. Smile sweetly and leave the room while your friend opens and closes his or her mouth in horror, looking a bit like . . . well, a goldfish!

HOW TO MAKE A SLED GO FASTER

Here are some essential tips for safe and speedy sledding.

While you need boots with a good grip to keep you from slipping in icy weather, you want the opposite when it comes to your sled. The smoother the base of your sled, the better. The best way to reduce friction between your sled and the snow is to rub the underside with candle wax, vegetable oil, or furniture polish.

You'll pick up the fastest speeds on areas of ground where the snow is really packed down. Going down the same path several times will do the trick, or follow in the tracks of people who started sledding before you.

SAFETY TIPS

- Get permission first, and make sure an adult knows where you're sledding or accompanies you.

- Dress warmly and wear a helmet.

- Sled only in a safe area. Avoid roads, driveways, trees, and cliff tops!

- Sit or lie on the sled with your feet pointing downhill.

- Don't sled in the dark or when it is icy.

- Don't sled straight into a large mound of snow unless you know the area well. It might hide a tree stump or barbed wire.

- Learn how to make a sharp turn or stop your sled by dragging your feet.

Tip: If your sled won't stop or you're out of control, roll off it onto the ground. Don't worry about your sled. You can get it once it stops sliding.

HOW TO KNOW WHICH COLORS TO WEAR

The secret to finding clothes that suit you is to decide whether your coloring is warm or cool. This mini questionnaire will help you find out.

WHAT COLOR ARE YOUR EYES?

Take a mirror over to the window when the daylight is good and have a close look at the color of your eyes. Are they:

a. Golden brown, green, green-blue, turquoise, or hazel with gold or brown flecks?

b. Deep brown or black-brown, gray-blue, dark blue, or hazel with white, gray, or blue flecks?

WHAT IS YOUR SKIN TONE?

Go back to the mirror and check out the color of your skin. Pay particular attention to the skin along your jawline. Is it:

a. Brown with pink or golden undertones, pale with peach or gold undertones, freckled, or golden brown?

b. Very dark brown, olive, pale, or medium with faint pink undertones or no color in your cheeks?

WHAT IS YOUR HAIR COLOR?

Now take a look at your hair color. Is it:

a. Deep brown with gold or red highlights, red, or strawberry blond?

b. Blue-black, deep coffee brown, medium ash brown, medium golden brown, ash blond, or golden blond?

ARE YOU WARM OR COOL?

If you answered mostly *a*'s, your coloring is warm. You will look great in earth tones. This means golden browns, yellows, orange-based reds, rich pinks, and rich greens.

If your answers were mostly *b*'s, your coloring is cool. You will look great in jewel tones. This means blues, clear greens, bright pinks, purples, and blue-based reds.

HOW TO LIVEN UP A SLEEPOVER

Here are two games that will add some laughter to any sleepover and are perfect for four or more friends to play together.

THE RING GAME

All you need for this game is a long piece of string (about 9 feet long) and a ring (the type that goes on a finger—any size will do). Slide the ring onto the string, then tie the ends of the string together to create a giant loop.

Choose one player to stand in the middle of the string loop. The other players stand in a circle around this person, holding the string in their hands.

The player in the middle closes her eyes and counts to ten. Meanwhile, the other players pass the ring along the string, hiding it in their hands.

When the player in the middle has finished counting, she opens her eyes and has to try to guess where the ring is. While she is trying to guess, the other players can continue passing the ring from person to person. It's okay to pretend you're passing the ring even when you're not.

When the player in the middle eventually guesses correctly, she changes places with the person who was caught with the ring in her hand, and the game starts again.

THE KNIFE AND FORK GAME

This is possibly the best game in the world because it gives you the perfect excuse to eat chocolate.

Sit on the floor in a circle. Put a large bar of wrapped chocolate on a plate in the middle, with a knife and fork on either side, a pair of gloves, a hat, and a scarf.

Starting with the youngest player, take turns rolling a single die. As soon as someone throws a six, she must put on the hat, scarf, and gloves; grab the knife and fork; and start to eat the chocolate. The problem is the player is not allowed to touch the chocolate with her hands. Instead, she must use the fork to get the wrapper off and lift the chocolate into her mouth.

While this is going on, the other players continue to take turns rolling the die as quickly as they can. As soon as another six is thrown, the player eating the chocolate must stop and give the knife, fork, hat, gloves, and scarf to the person who threw the six. She puts them on and begins eating.

Play continues until the chocolate is all gone.

HOW TO BE AN EGYPTIAN QUEEN

Egyptian queens are said to have been beautiful and clever, but most of all they were incredibly powerful because people believed they were goddesses.

Here is how to make sure your friends and family recognize that, deep down, you are an Egyptian queen, too.

ROYAL TREATMENT

- Avoid the risk of being poisoned by rival royals who are eager to get their hands on your crown. Get a servant to taste your food before you eat anything (a younger brother is ideal). Tell the person who cooked your food that you don't mean to be rude, but you can't risk it.

- Insist on writing all your homework in hieroglyphics on rolls of papyrus (the stuff ancient Egyptians used to write on). It will take time, but your history teacher will be seriously impressed.

- Arrange all your possessions in a pyramid shape in the middle of your bedroom.

• Make a papier-mâché headdress with a cobra's head at the front. This was the height of Egyptian fashion in royal circles. Float around in a white tunic, strappy sandals, and dozens of bracelets.

• Wear heavy black eyeliner and green eye shadow. When applying the eyeliner, use the picture below for inspiration.

• Insist your parents build an obelisk in the backyard. This is a tall, narrow monument with a pyramid shape at the top.

• Demand that four friends pick up your chair and carry you when you head to the mall.

HOW TO MAKE YOUR OWN CANDY

There's no need to head to the candy store when you can make your very own candy. It makes a wonderful gift for friends and family.

COCONUT CANDY

You Will Need:

- 14-ounce can sweetened condensed milk
- a large bowl
- 1 1/2 cups confectioners' sugar
- a sieve
- 12 ounces shredded coconut
- a loaf pan
- plastic wrap
- 1/2 teaspoon red food coloring

WHAT YOU DO

1. Pour the condensed milk into a large bowl. Sift in the confectioners' sugar by putting it in a sieve placed over the bowl and tapping the side of the sieve with your hand.

2. Add the shredded coconut and stir until there are no dry pieces of coconut left.

3. Line a loaf pan with some plastic wrap and spread half the mixture in the bottom of the pan.

4. Add the red coloring to the mixture left in the bowl and stir until it is an even color all the way through.

5. Spread the pink mixture on top of the white mixture in the loaf pan, then place in the refrigerator overnight to set.

6. When the mixture has set, invert the pan to remove it. Then remove the plastic wrap and cut the candy into squares.

PEPPERMINT CREAMS

Delicious and full of minty flavor, peppermint creams make the perfect partners for your coconut candy.

You Will Need:

- 1 egg white
- a mixing bowl
- 1/2 teaspoon peppermint extract
- 1/2 teaspoon green food coloring
- a heatproof glass bowl
- 2 cups confectioners' sugar
- rolling pin
- 3.5 ounces milk chocolate
- a pan
- a baking sheet covered with foil

WHAT YOU DO

1. Get an adult to help you separate the egg white from the yolk. Pour the white into the mixing bowl with the peppermint extract and green food coloring. Mix well.

2. Now sift the confectioners' sugar into the bowl and stir until the ingredients combine to form a smooth ball. Add a little more confectioners' sugar if the mixture is too sticky.

3. Dust a work surface with a little confectioners' sugar and roll the mixture into a long sausage shape.

4. Slice the roll into pieces about 1/4 inch thick and place on a board to dry.

5. Melt the chocolate. You can do this by breaking it into squares and placing them in a heatproof glass bowl. Place the bowl over a pan of barely simmering water and stir until the chocolate has melted. (Ask an adult to help you with this.)

6. Dip one side of each peppermint cream into the melted chocolate. Place each candy on the foil-covered sheet to set.

HOW TO PUT ON A SHOE BOX-THEATER SHOW

Thrill your family and friends with a show that's all about them.

THE THEATER

Start by making your theater out of an old shoe box.

1. Stand the shoe box on one of its long sides and cut an opening like a window at each of the short ends. These openings are where your "actors" will enter the stage.

2. Decide where your play is going to be set, such as in a house, a school, or by the ocean. Make a scenery backdrop for your

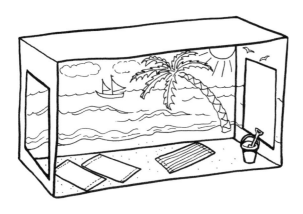

theater by cutting a sheet of paper that will fit snugly into the back of the shoe box. Then you can either draw the scenery or use magazine pictures. You could even use family photographs cut out and stuck to the paper, but ask an adult first.

3. Add any extra bits to your "set" that you like. You might want to include some cardboard trees, dollhouse furniture, or fancy felt floors.

4. Use two thin pieces of fabric (each two-thirds of the width of your stage) to create a pair of curtains at the front of the theater. Make two holes on either side of the stage, just beneath the roof. Tie a piece of string between the holes. Fold the top of each piece of fabric over the string and then secure it with a simple running stitch (see page 34) about a finger's width below the string. Check that your curtains open and close properly.

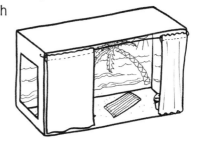

THE CAST

Cut out the faces of your family and friends from old photographs (always ask permission first). Stick them onto bodies cut from the cardboard of the shoe-box lid. With felt-tip pens, draw costumes on the bodies.

Use masking tape to attach your "actors" to straws or sticks. One end of the stick should be stuck sideways across the back of the body so you can use the stick "handle" to move the actor from the sides of the stage. Remember that some characters will come in on the right-hand side of the stage and some from the left, so attach the handles accordingly.

Tip: You'll need a friend or two to help you if you're going to have more than two characters on stage at any one time.

WRITE YOUR SHOW

Write a simple script that's based on a real event in your characters' lives. Perhaps it's a birthday party, a day on the beach, or something funny that happened in school. If you don't want to write it down, spend a few minutes thinking about your story before you begin.

TIPS FOR A FABULOUS SHOW

- Use people's real nicknames.

- If someone, like your dad, has a favorite saying, include that in the show. Everyone will recognize it and laugh.

- Try to include a few jokes.

- Keep your story really simple, with a beginning, middle, and an end.

- Think about including a song and dance at the end as it's always a crowd-pleaser.

HOW TO REMOVE A RING THAT'S STUCK

Have you ever tried on a friend's ring that's too small and gotten it stuck? If it happens again, don't panic. Just follow these steps and the ring will be off in no time.

1. Cool It. Fill a bowl with cold water and add some ice. Hold your hand in the ice water for ten seconds (or as long as you can bear to). This will help reduce any swelling in your finger.

2. Oil It. Rub plenty of hand cream, olive oil, or dishwashing liquid in and around the ring and up the length of your finger.

3. Twist It. Gently twist (don't yank) the ring as you slowly work it up and over the knuckle of your finger.

HOW TO SALUTE THE SUN

If you've never tried yoga, this is a great place to start. First, ask an adult if it's okay for you to try these poses. The sun salutation is a series of twelve yoga asanas, or poses, to stretch your body, calm your mind, and really get you ready for the day.

These moves should all flow naturally from one to another, so make sure you do them all in the right order.

Take your time and keep practicing. Make sure you stretch gently and stretch only as far as is comfortable. If any of the movements hurts, stop right away.

THE SUN SALUTATION

1. Stand with your feet together, hands in front of your chest as though you're praying. Breathe in gently and raise your arms, straightening your elbows.

2. Bend backward, raising your arms to the sky, palms facing each other, allowing your eyes to look up and back. You should bend back only as far as is comfortable.

3. Breathe out and fold forward from the hips with a straight back. Keep your knees straight but not locked (don't worry if you can't reach the floor).

4. Breathe in and step your right foot back, resting your knee on the floor. Look forward.

5. Breathe out and bring your left foot back to join your right foot. Support your body on your hands and your toes, keeping your back straight. This is called the Plank.

6. Breathe out as you lower your knees, chest, and chin to the ground. Keep your elbows in at your sides as your arms bend.

7. Breathing in, arch your back and stretch your head and neck upward, relaxing the shoulders. This is called the Cobra.

8. Breathe out, straighten your arms, and push yourself back so your bottom is in the air and your back and legs are straight. This is known as the Downward Dog.

9. Breathe in as you step your right foot forward and place it between your hands.

10. Breathing out, step your left foot next to your right foot. Straighten your legs as you bend forward and touch the floor next to your feet.

11. As you breathe in, reach your arms forward, and then gently bend backward. Keep your arms straight and close to your ears. Bend back only as far as is comfortable.

12. Breathe out and return to the very first position, gradually bringing your arms down. Finish with your hands in front of you in the prayer position.

HOW TO MAKE AN APRIL FOOLS' MEAL

The first day of April is also known as April Fools' Day and it's a great day to play practical jokes on your family and friends. Tricks with food are always real winners.

Here are some ideas to turn mealtime into trick time. Make sure you prepare your tricks well in advance. Invite your guests to your April Fools' meal, then sit back and watch the fun.

FOOD FUN

- If your milk comes in cartons, turn it blue with a few drops of food coloring. It's harmless, and your guests won't notice until they pour it out.

- If your family eats O-shaped cereal, thread the O's onto a piece of string and put them back in the box.

- Make a fake fried egg. Arrange a spoonful of plain yogurt in an oval on a plate. Place an apricot half in the middle. Serve it to your family with a strip of real bacon.

- Make some Jell-O following the instructions on the box. Before it sets, pour the Jell-O into glasses. Place a straw in each one and put in the fridge. Wait until the Jell-O sets before you serve your "fruit punch." Watch your guests try to drink it!

- Put an empty eggshell upside down in an egg cup and surprise someone with a boiled egg that has nothing inside.

- Scoop a small hole in an apple with the end of a spoon and insert a sweet gummy worm — yuck!

- Serve scoops of mashed potatoes in ice cream cones and tell your guests it's vanilla ice cream.

- With a pin, pierce several holes in a drinking straw, then place the straw in a glass of fruit juice.

- Put plastic wrap over the top of glasses of milk and watch the confusion as your guests put them to their lips.

- Put salt in the sugar bowl and sugar in the salt shaker.

- Scrape out the icing from the middle of a sandwich cookie and replace it with toothpaste.

Tip: Some people say that on April 1 you have only until midday to make your April Fools' joke. If you play a practical joke after midday, the joke's on you. Other people say it's fine to play tricks all day long.

HOW TO PRETEND YOU'RE A SURFER GIRL

It's easy to convince people you're a surfer girl without ever setting foot in the water. You just need to get the look and talk the talk.

LOOK RIGHT

Surfer girls dress cool and casual. It's about looking relaxed and sporty rather than dressing up to impress boys.

- Base your look around shorts and a bikini top. Add a few layers of faded T-shirts (ones with sailor stripes or seaside images are particularly great). Finish the look with a colorful hoodie.

- Flip-flops and loads of friendship bracelets are essential.

- Consider borrowing a wet suit and having it draped casually over your shoulders so it looks as though you are going to hit the beach later.

Tip: Surfer girls' hair always looks beautifully tousled or rumpled by the sun, sea, and sand. Get the effect by mixing two tablespoons of salt in two cups of warm water. Pour it over your hair after shampooing and don't rinse it out. This salty rinse will give your hair an authentic beach-babe look.

TALK RIGHT

Learn some essential "surf speak." As you grow in confidence, try dropping a few of the following phrases into your conversation to convince people you're a bona fide surfer girl.

Deck: The part of the surfboard you stand on.

Quiver: A surfer's collection of surfboards.

Carve a Wave: This is the classic surfing move where you make wiggly turns when you are surfing on a wave.

Impact Zone: The place where the waves are breaking.

The Soup: The white foamy water created when a wave has broken.

Dropping In: Sneaking onto a wave that's already occupied by another surfer. This is the quickest way to make a surfer angry with you.

Stink Eye: A mean stare normally given when another surfer's done something bad, like dropping into your wave.

Tube: This is when a wave breaks over the top of you so you're surfing inside a cylindrical hole. It's every surfer's dream come true.

Green Room: The inside of a tube.

Riptide: A really strong and potentially dangerous current under the water.

Wipeout: This is where you fall off your surfboard in spectacular style!

Grommet: A young surfer.

HOW TO MAKE PAPER SNOWFLAKES

Paper snowflakes are easy to make and look really good. You can stick them on windows, hang them from the ceiling, or stick them on your front door in a circle shape to create a Christmas wreath.

You Will Need:

- some plain white paper (a square 8 inches by 8 inches for a large snowflake and 4 inches by 4 inches for a smaller one)
- scissors
- a pencil
- glue
- glitter

HOW TO DO IT

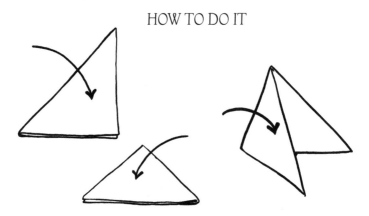

1. Fold the square in half diagonally. Then fold it in half diagonally again.

2. Now fold one point two-thirds of the way across the base of your triangle to achieve the shape shown above.

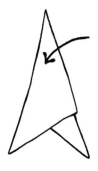

3. Fold the other point across as shown here.

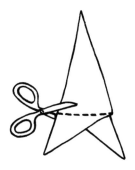

4. Cut off the two points as shown here.

5. Using a pencil, draw zigzags along the long sides of the triangle shape. The more zigzags you draw, the more delicate and decorative your snowflake will be. Use scissors to cut along your pencil lines.

6. Unfold your snowflake and admire the finished result!

Tip: Make your snowflake sparkle with some glue and glitter.

HOW TO PLAY WINK MURDER

Wink Murder is the perfect spooky game for a Halloween party.

HOW TO PLAY

Grab at least four friends and sit in a circle. Deal one playing card facedown for each person who is playing — one of the cards must be the ace of spades.

Each player looks at her card (without showing it to anyone else). The person who has the ace of spades is the murderer!

The players sit in silence, looking at one another. The murderer kills a victim by winking at her without anyone else noticing. When a player has been winked at, she must "die." She can scream dramatically or just fall to the floor, as long as she makes it clear to the other players that she is dead.

The murderer wins if she kills all the other players. She loses if someone spots her and correctly accuses her of being the murderer before everyone is dead.

HOW TO THROW A SURPRISE PARTY

If you want to make one of your friends happy and shocked at the same time, throw a surprise party for her next birthday. There's more to organizing a surprise party than blowing up a few balloons. Here are ten golden rules to follow.

TEN GOLDEN RULES

Rule One: Decide the date. It's important to know that your guest of honor will be available, so check with her family and friends first to make sure she isn't doing something else that day.

Rule Two: Decide on a fake activity that your guest of honor will believe she is doing on the day of the party.

Rule Three: Send out invitations that make it very clear the party is to be a surprise. You can't emphasize this enough to people. Invite them to come half an hour before the star guest.

Rule Four: If you see or speak to the guest of honor on the big day, be really offhand with her and ignore the fact that it's her birthday. Even if she mentions that it's her birthday, act disinterested. It will make the surprise even better later on.

Rule Five: Get the music, food, and drinks ready. Make sure they're the guest of honor's favorites.

Rule Six: If the guest of honor is someone who lives in your house, make sure you hide all evidence of the party.

Rule Seven: When the other guests arrive, store all their bags and coats out of view so it isn't obvious that there are other people at your house.

Rule Eight: Make sure you choose one friend to act as a lookout. He or she should give a signal to warn all your guests to be quiet when the guest of honor arrives outside the house.

Rule Nine: Switch off the music so your guest arrives to a quiet, ordinary-looking house.

Rule Ten: When your guest of honor walks in, switch on the lights and the music, and get everyone to shout "SURPRISE!" Pick him or her up off the floor and let the party begin!

HOW TO WRAP A PRESENT BEAUTIFULLY

The only thing more exciting than unwrapping a present is unwrapping a present that looks totally gorgeous. Here are some simple dos and don'ts on how to up the "oooh" factor.

DO work on a large, flat, clear area. If it's the floor, sweep it first, as little bits of grit can easily tear wrapping paper.

DON'T use too much paper, as it will be difficult to make neat folds when wrapping.

DO place the present in the middle of the sheet of wrapping paper. This will help you create evenly sized folds at either end of the gift.

DON'T struggle to wrap paper around an awkwardly shaped present. Put the gift in a box first. This will make it easier to wrap.

DO tear several pieces of tape off the roll before you start. Stick one end on a smooth, hard object, such as the edge of a table, so that you can just reach for a piece easily when you need it.

DON'T forget to wrap the paper tightly around your gift. Make sharp creases when you fold the paper.

DO use a heavy object such as a paperweight or a can of beans to keep the flaps in place before you tape them.

DON'T use ordinary ribbon if you want to create a bow. Use wire-edged ribbon instead, as it will hold the shape of the bow perfectly.

DO attach a tag that says the gift is from you.

GET CRAFTY AND CREATIVE

Once you've got the basics right, you can get really creative and wrap presents in a truly individual way.

• Think beyond ordinary wrapping paper. You could use cartoon pages from a comic, musical scores, maps, or posters. Why not try to match the style of paper to the interests of the person who is receiving the gift?

• Decorate plain wrapping paper by painting it with food coloring. This works much better than ordinary poster paints as it doesn't flake when the paper is folded.

• Presents look great when wrapped in a piece of pretty fabric and tied with a ribbon.

• Why not brighten up plain paper by adding sparkly stickers, or dab on some glue and sprinkle it with glitter or confetti? Pasting on feathers works well, too.

• Brown paper and string always look sophisticated wrapped neatly around a present. You could use a luggage label for the gift tag.

• Turn a small, odd-shaped gift into something special by stuffing the gift into a paper tube (a paper-towel roll is ideal). Wrap the tube with brightly colored tissue paper and tie the ends with ribbon. Decorate with stickers.

HOW TO TELL A HAIRDRESSER WHAT YOU REALLY WANT

Most hairdressers are better at cutting hair than reading minds. So the next time you have your heart set on a new look, remember these golden rules.

PICTURE PERFECT

Don't be shy about tearing pictures out of magazines to show your hairdresser how you want your hair. This will give you a really good starting point for discussion. If you can't find a picture of what you want, cut out pictures of what you really don't want. This sounds strange, but it is helpful to show the stylist your dislikes as well as your likes.

SHOW, DON'T TELL

Use your fingers to show exactly how long or short you want your hair to be. That will help prevent the hairdresser from cutting a chunk off the bottom of your hair when all you really wanted was a trim.

DON'T USE "HAIRDRESSER SPEAK"

Do you really know the differences among "layering," "thinning," and "feathering"? If you use a term incorrectly, the hairdresser may go ahead and give you something completely different from what you had in mind. Describe what you want with simple words and gestures so you can be sure you get the look you want.

HOW TO MAKE A CORK HORSE

These cute little cork horses look great on a bedroom windowsill. They're so easy to construct, you might be tempted to make a whole herd.

You Will Need:

- a cork
- a craft knife
- a piece of sturdy cardboard
- a felt-tip pen
- scissors
- glue
- four toothpicks
- yarn

WHAT YOU DO

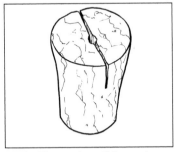

1. The cork will form the horse's body. Make a slit with a sharp craft knife in one end, ready for the head. (Ask an adult for help with this.)

2. Carefully draw a horse's head and neck in profile on the cardboard. Cut it out. Color in both sides of the cardboard, adding as much horsey detail as you like.

72

3. Dab some glue onto the end of the neck and slide it into the slit in the cork.

4. Use the four toothpicks to form the legs. Push them into the cork body, taking care to get them nicely balanced so your horse stands up straight.

5. Cut some lengths of yarn and glue them onto the horse to form a mane and tail.

Tip: Try turning your horse into a zebra by drawing black stripes on the cork and using black and white yarn.

HOW TO EAT YOUR FRUITS AND VEGETABLES

If you want to stay healthy on the inside and gorgeous on the outside, you need to eat at least five servings of fruits and vegetables a day. Two servings of fruit and three of vegetables is a great place to start. If you're one of those people who don't like fruits and vegetables, here's how to sneak them into your diet.

- Freeze fruit smoothies to make yummy ice pops.

- Thread pieces of fruit onto a wooden skewer to make a vitamin-packed "kebab." Dip it into yogurt or chocolate sauce.

- Scatter loads of finely chopped veggies on top of your favorite store-bought pizza before it goes in the oven.

- Sip a carton of fresh fruit juice at lunch instead of a soda.

- Dip raw chunks of vegetables such as carrots, celery, and cauliflower into your favorite dips instead of potato chips.

- Toss a handful of fresh or frozen fruit over your ice cream.

- Scatter dried banana chips into your morning cereal.

- Spread peanut butter on the inside of a piece of celery, then sprinkle with raisins to make "ants on a log."

- Skewer grapes, pineapple, and cheese onto toothpicks for a perfect party treat.

- Try a new fruit or vegetable! Persuade your parents to buy one exotic fruit or vegetable you've never tried each week.

HOW TO GROW AN APPLE TREE FROM A SEED

1. Eat your apple and carefully extract the seeds.

2. Fill a plant pot with some soil. If you don't have a plant pot, an old food container will do.

3. Push several seeds into the soil, making sure the soil covers them. Water well.

4. Cover the top of the pot with a loose-fitting lid and leave the pot in a nice warm place for several weeks. Water from time to time to make sure the soil doesn't dry out.

5. Once your seeds start to sprout into shoots, identify the strongest-looking one and pick out the rest.

6. Keep the shoot watered and in a sunny spot and watch it grow.

HOW TO SURVIVE A CHARGING ELEPHANT

If you're unfortunate enough to come face-to-face with an angry elephant, it's useful to know what to do.

EMERGENCY TACTICS

- Always stay downwind of the elephant. To do this you must figure out the direction the wind is blowing. You want the wind to be blowing past the elephant and toward you. This will make it harder for the elephant to pick up your scent, and as elephants have bad eyesight, it will help you remain unnoticed.

- Learn to recognize the difference between an elephant that is making a "mock charge" and one that is serious about chasing you. Unfortunately, the art of reading elephants' body language can take many years to perfect, and you may get squashed before you learn it. If the elephant's ears are

relaxed, it is probably only pretending to charge. If you stay very still, it will probably lose interest in you. However, if the elephant fans out its ears and shakes them, the charge is probably for real.

• If you have to run for it, try moving in sharp zigzags. Elephants find it hard to change direction quickly thanks to their huge bulk.

• Don't think that setting a mouse on the elephant will make the elephant run away. Elephants are not really afraid of rodents.

• Don't be tempted to jump into water to escape, as elephants are good swimmers. Climb a tree instead, but be sure to check the tree for leopards first.

• If you're running for it and the elephant is getting closer, throw a decoy for it to attack. Your jacket or a large branch will work, but a huge sack of peanuts would be even better!

HOW TO MAKE YOUR OWN HERBAL TEA

Fresh or dried herbs can be used to make a cup of delicious herbal tea. All you need to do is add water!

You can pick fresh herbs from the garden, grow them on a windowsill, or buy them in bunches from the supermarket. You will need a teaspoon of dried herbs or 3 teaspoons of roughly chopped fresh herbs for 1 cup of tea. Mint works really well and is particularly easy to grow.

MAKING MINT TEA

1. Place 3 teaspoons of roughly chopped mint leaves in a teapot, a pitcher, or a special coffee pot that has a plunger. Pour freshly boiled water over the leaves (ask an adult for help).

2. Leave to infuse for five minutes before you strain and serve the tea.

If you don't like having little bits of leaf floating in your tea, why not make your own herbal teabags?

HOMEMADE HERBAL TEA BAGS

Cut a small square of muslin that is around 4 inches by 4 inches. Place your herbs in the middle, then gather up the edges. Tie tightly with string, leaving the ends long enough to let you dangle the teabag in a cup.

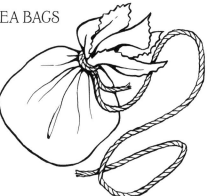

HEALING HERBS

Herbs taste delicious, and many have healing properties, too. But don't use just any old herbs. It's important to check that they're safe to use first. The two best ones to try are peppermint and chamomile.

Peppermint. As well as tasting fresh and delicious, peppermint tea can help soothe a stomachache and might make you breathe a little more easily when you have a cold.

Chamomile. This herb has a lovely taste and makes a great bedtime tea, as it's said to help you sleep.

SUN TEA

How about treating yourself to a cup of sun tea on a hot day?

Simply fill a clean jar with cold water, throw in a handful of your favorite crushed fresh herbs, and leave it in the sun for three or four hours. Stir in a little honey to sweeten, pour over ice, and enjoy. Delicious!

HOW TO MAKE THE PERFECT DAISY CHAIN

There's no nicer way to while away a summer afternoon in the park than by making daisy chains. You can create necklaces, bracelets, crowns, leis, ankle bracelets, or rings. Whatever you go for, make sure yours are the prettiest with these tips.

PERFECT CHAINS

1. Pick daisies that have long, strong stalks (be sure to ask for permission first). Pick them close to the root so you have plenty of stem to work with.

2. Use your thumbnail to split the stalk lengthwise. Create a slit that's around 1/2 inch long and about 1/4 inch from the end.

3. Thread the stalk of a second daisy through the slit you've created and pull all the way through up to the flower head.

4. Make a slit in the stalk of the second daisy and repeat. Keep going until your daisy chain is as long as you would like it to be.

5. When you're ready to finish, make a long slit in the stalk of your final daisy and fit the entire head of your first flower through it. Pull gently to tighten.

TOP DAISY TIPS

- You can dry daisy chains by hanging them in a warm, dry place at home.

- Don't limit yourself to daisies – buttercups and poppies work well, too. (Only pick wildflowers that are very common. Never pick a wildflower unless there are at least eight other healthy specimens around it that you leave unpicked.)

- Think about the final effect you're after. For a chain that's dense in flowers (ideal for a crown), split the stalk close to the bloom. For a more spaced-out look, split the stalk closer to the root.

HOW TO MAKE DELICIOUS SANDWICH COOKIES

These cookies are so good they'll seem to melt in your mouth. You can eat them one at a time, but they are even better sandwiched together with icing in the middle.

You Will Need:

- a bowl
- 3/4 cup soft butter
- 1/2 cup confectioners' sugar
- a sieve
- 3/4 cup all-purpose flour
- 1/2 cup cornstarch
- 1/2 teaspoon baking powder
- a pinch of salt
- a greased baking sheet
- a fork
- oven mitts

For icing:
- 1/2 cup soft butter
- 1/2 cup confectioners' sugar

WHAT TO DO

1. Preheat the oven to 350°F. (Ask an adult to supervise whenever you use an oven.)

2. In a bowl, mix together the butter and confectioners' sugar until the mixture is nice and smooth.

3. Use a sieve to sift the flour, cornstarch, and baking powder into the bowl. Add the pinch of salt, too.

4. Carefully fold the dry ingredients into the butter mixture.

5. Take 1 teaspoon of mixture at a time and roll it into a ball.

6. Place on a greased baking sheet and press down the top of each ball with the prongs of a fork to flatten it a little.

7. Bake in the oven for 15 to 18 minutes or until the cookies are lightly golden. Use oven mitts when you take them out of the oven. Let them cool on a rack.

8. In another bowl, mix together the butter and confectioners' sugar for the icing. Spread the bottom of one cookie with a teaspoon of the butter icing mixture, then press another cookie on top.

HOW TO HAVE PERFECT POSTURE

Check your posture in a mirror and follow these dos and don'ts.

- **DO** hold your neck straight from your hairline to your shoulders.

- **DON'T** let your head jut forward and your neck curve. You should be able to balance a book on your head.

- **DO** relax your shoulders and keep your shoulder blades flat.

- **DON'T** let your chest cave in. Pull your shoulders out and back, but don't let them rise toward your ears.

- **DO** keep your spine straight with just a small curve in the small of your back, not a deep hollow.

- **DO** tuck in your butt and pull in your stomach.

- **DON'T** let your feet splay out or turn in.

HOW TO SPOT A MOVIE CLICHÉ

Next time you and your friends sit down to enjoy a movie night with popcorn, try renting a high school movie. Then see how many of the following clichés you can spot.

- There are always lots of pretty girls who are mean and selfish.

- No one has lots of pimples.

- Football players ALWAYS go out with cheerleaders.

- Girls wear special makeup that never rubs off or smudges. It's only the mean girl whose mascara runs when she cries.

- When everyone in the school starts to sing, there is always music playing that everyone dances to, and everyone always knows exactly what steps to do.

- Whenever children are left alone at home, something goes wrong.

- When there is trouble, the heroine will tell a younger kid to hide and stay hidden until it is safe to come out. The little kid never obeys and is always captured by the bad guys.

- If there is a fight or a chase, kids can usually escape from adults by crawling between their legs.

- Boys and girls who have been friends for years will suddenly realize how gorgeous the other person is and fall head over heels in love.

- There is always a high school prom at which mean girls get punished and heroines have a great time.

HOW TO PUT TOGETHER A MAKEUP BAG

There's nothing wrong with looking good while you're on the go. There are a few things worth taking with you whenever you travel, whether it's to school or on a trip.

IN THE BAG

Grab yourself a pretty little bag to store your stash in. Something the size of a pencil case will do perfectly. Now you are ready to collect the following items:

- A mini mirror is great for close-up beauty repairs. It's also perfect for seeing what's going on behind you in class!

- A pack of tissues for blotting shiny skin and wiping a runny nose.

- Lip balm is great for keeping lips soft and smooth. Choose the cream type that comes in a little tube. You can also rub a tiny dot into your nails and cuticles to keep them strong.

- Medicated pimple cream is essential if your skin's prone to sudden breakouts.

- A mini makeup brush. Use it to apply pimple cream as using your fingers will just spread infection.

- A mini hairbrush will keep your hair neat and tidy.

- Wind a couple of hair bands around the handle of your brush in case you want to pull your hair back into a ponytail later on.

- Carry a couple of pretty hair clips so that you can add pizzazz in an instant.

HOW TO MAKE A DISCO MIRROR BALL

A mirror ball is a great way to give any party some extra sparkle. Just follow these easy steps to make your own.

You Will Need:

- a round balloon
- petroleum jelly
- 1 cup flour
- 2 cups water
- some newspapers
- a pin
- a thick paintbrush
- black acrylic or poster paint
- scissors
- silver mirror cardboard (you can get this from a craft store)
- glue

88

- a large needle and some thick thread
- sticky putty
- masking tape

Make a Papier-Mâché Ball. Blow up a round balloon to make a nice ball shape. Spread a thin layer of petroleum jelly all over the surface of the balloon (this will make it easier to remove the balloon later). Mix the flour and water thoroughly to form a thick paste.

Tear up lots of strips of newspaper and stick them onto the balloon using plenty of the flour paste. Leave a big enough space at the top of the balloon to fit your hand through.

Cover the balloon with at least four layers of newspaper, letting each layer dry before starting a new one.

Leave your papier-mâché ball to dry completely.

Then use a pin to pop the balloon and pull it out of the ball.

Paint the Ball Black. Use a paintbrush and black acrylic or poster paint to cover all the newspaper on the ball. Leave to dry again.

Add Silver Squares. Cut the silver mirror cardboard into lots of squares about 1 inch by 1 inch. Cover the ball in the squares using the glue. Arrange the squares in nice neat rows, trimming any to fit awkward spaces. Your aim is to cover the entire ball, like a mosaic. When finished, you should be able to see only a tiny bit of black paint peeking through.

Attach the Thread. Use a thick needle to pierce three holes about 1 inch below the opening of your ball. Space them at equal distances around the rim. It's a good idea to hold a ball of sticky putty on the inside of the ball where you are making the hole to prevent you from sticking the needle through your finger!

Feed a length of thick thread through the needle and make sure you tie a big knot at the end. From the inside of the ball, feed the needle through one of the holes. Use masking tape to secure the knot to the inside of the ball. Repeat for each hole in your ball.

Party Time. Finally, ask an adult to help you hang up your mirror ball using the three threads. Give it a spin, and let the disco begin!

HOW TO PLAY THE FLOUR TOWER GAME

The Flour Tower Game is perfect for two or more players. It is probably best to play this one in the kitchen or the backyard since it can be messy!

You Will Need:

- a shallow bowl
- flour
- a spoon
- a wooden board (a cutting board or breadboard will do)
- a piece of candy or chocolate

THE RULES

1. Fill the bowl to the brim with flour, squishing the flour down hard with a spoon.

2. Put the wooden board over the top of the bowl and carefully flip them upside down. Do this by holding one hand on top of the board and the other on the bottom of the bowl. The bowl should end up upside down on top of the board.

3. Carefully lift the bowl so that you're left with a bowl-shaped dome of flour on top of the wooden board.

4. Place the piece of candy or chocolate on top of the flour dome.

5. Each player takes a turn scooping away some flour with the spoon without disturbing the piece of candy. This is easy to start with, but it soon gets more and more difficult as the flour is cut away, leaving a skinny tower with the piece of candy on top.

6. The player who makes the flour tower collapse and the piece of candy fall is the loser. Her punishment is to pick the piece of candy from the middle of the flour with her teeth — no hands allowed!

HOW TO MAKE A GARDEN ON A TRAY

You can have a whole garden on your bedroom windowsill if you create it on a tray. The basic method is described here, but your garden's individual look totally depends on what you find to put in it.

GETTING STARTED

A gardener's seedling tray will make an ideal base for your garden, but any container that's around 20 inches by 10 inches and at least 2 inches deep will work well.

Prepare the tray by lining the bottom of it with a sheet of plastic (using an old plastic bag works well). Cover the plastic with a fine layer of gravel (to help with drainage) and on top of that, spread a thick layer of soil.

CREATING THE LANDSCAPE

Plants. Small houseplants, mini cacti, or flowers will be great as the main plants in your garden. Simply make a hole in the soil, put in the plants, and pat them into place.

Pond. A small mirror or circle of aluminum foil makes a great pond. Cut tiny fish out of orange paper to "swim" in it.

Rocks. Use pretty pebbles or stones to create mountains or boulders.

Grass. Moss from a garden store or from your backyard makes great grass. If you can't find any, cut shapes out of green felt.

Pathway. Carefully use some gravel or bark chippings to create a path in your garden. Make it as twisty as you like.

THE FINISHING TOUCHES

It's the small details that will bring your mini garden to life.

- Add mini figures of people or animals enjoying your garden.

  - Various dollhouse items work well. A seat could be a garden bench, ornaments could be garden statues, and a carpet could be a picnic blanket.

- Make a "clothesline" with two Popsicle sticks and some string and hang some dolls' clothes from it.

- Make a garden shed with a small box painted brown.

- Create a snowy effect by sprinkling your garden with salt. Or a snowman made from white modeling clay.

  - Add some train track at the bottom of the garden with a train running along it.

HOW TO BREAK BAD BEAUTY HABITS

It's often the simplest things that give your looks a boost, and the simplest things that can ruin them, too. Here's the lowdown on the bad beauty habits it is time to break.

Constantly Touching Your Face. All you're doing is rubbing grime from your fingertips onto your skin, which encourages pimples and blemishes.

Twiddling Your Hair. If you absentmindedly play with your hair all the time, you're on a fast track to split ends.

Licking Your Lips. The truth is, licking your lips actually makes them drier and more prone to chapping. Keep a delicious lip balm handy and reach for it when your lips feel dry.

Rubbing Your Eyes. The skin around your eyes is very thin and delicate. Constantly rubbing it can leave it red and sore.

Picking Pimples. When you pick at a pimple, you risk scarring and spreading infection. Dab on a clay-based face mask or an overnight pimple cream to dry it out.

Using Rubber Bands in Your Hair. Uncovered rubber bands tear and split your hair. Use a fabric-coated band instead. Rub a dot of conditioner onto the band beforehand to protect your hair while you wear it.

Nibbling Your Nails. It's a hard habit to break, but worth it if you want nice-looking hands. Try leaving one nail for biting and painting the rest with a yucky-tasting no-bite formula. As you gradually break the biting habit, paint the nail you left for biting, too.

Borrowing Makeup. You might be desperate to share your friend's eyeliner pencil, but do you want to share her eye infection, too?

Sleeping with the Heat on High. If you don't want skin like a crocodile, try sleeping in a cooler room. Turn the heat down before bed. Central heat makes the air so dry it'll sponge up moisture from your skin. If your parents insist on keeping the house warm, keep a well-watered plant in your room to keep the air moist.

Using Heated Hairstyling Appliances Every Day. Curling irons, straighteners, and even hair dryers are fine every now and again, but used every day they'll wreak havoc on your poor locks. Use them only on dry hair, and protect your hair with a blow-dry spray before using. Let your hair dry naturally whenever you can to keep it shiny and healthy.

HOW TO PLAY CAT'S CRADLE

Grab a friend and try out this string game. See how quickly you can perform the sequence.

HOW TO PLAY

1. Tie a piece of string that is about 60 inches long into a loop.

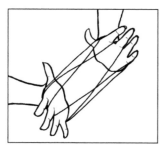

2. Slip both your hands, except your thumbs, inside the loop. Wrap the string around each hand again. With your middle finger, hook the string that lies across the opposite palm from underneath and pull. Repeat with the other hand to make a Cat's Cradle.

3. Using both her thumbs and index fingers, your friend should pinch the Cat's Cradle from above at the two points where the strings crisscross.

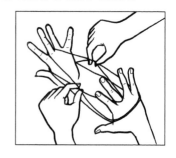

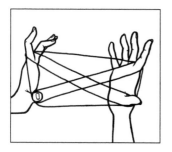

4. Your partner pulls the crosses out and around the outside strings. Then she scoops them up through the center. Let the cradle go so that she can pull it tight on her fingers. This is the Soldier's Bed.

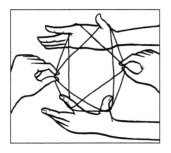

5. In exactly the same way, you must pinch the two points on the Soldier's Bed where the long strings cross.

6. Scoop them around and up through the center. As you draw the strings apart, they will form four parallel lines. This pattern is called Candles.

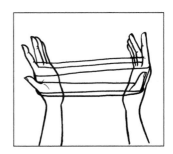

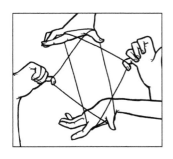

7. With the little finger of her right hand, your partner now hooks the string on the inside left, and with the little finger of her left hand, she hooks the string on the inside right.

8. Your partner then pushes her thumb and index fingers in the triangles, under the outside strings, and up the center, making a Reverse Cradle.

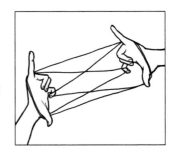

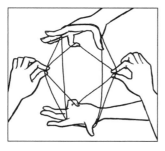

9. In the same way your friend made the Soldier's Bed, you must bring the crosses out and around the outside strings from underneath.

10. This time, turn your hands so your palms face down and push your fingers down into the open center before pulling taut.

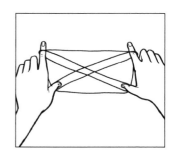

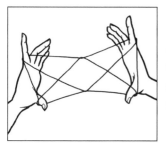

11. Your partner then repeats the actions you used to make Candles, but she magically creates a pattern of four triangles instead, called Cat's Eyes.

12. Now put your thumbs and index fingers down into each of the triangles, scoop up through the center and pull out to make a Fish in a Dish.

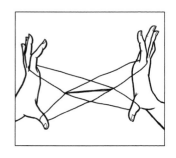

HOW TO MAKE PERFECT POPCORN

Turn a boring night in front of the TV into a fun movie night. Invite your friends over, switch on your favorite DVD, and enjoy a huge bowl of homemade popcorn.

Homemade popcorn takes minutes to make, tastes delicious, and costs much less than the ready-made or microwave stuff you can buy from the supermarket. You'll find popcorn kernels in a supermarket or health-food store.

All you need is a saucepan with a lid and an adult to help.

WHAT TO DO

1. Find the biggest saucepan in the house. It must have a lid. Put it on the stove and pour in a tablespoon of vegetable oil.

2. Add two handfuls of dry popcorn kernels or enough to just cover the bottom of the pan.

3. Give the pan a good shake to spread the oil around.

4. Put the lid on and turn the heat to medium.

5. Popcorn making requires patience. Don't be tempted to sneak a peek under the lid or you may get hit on the nose by a flying corn missile!

6. Soon you'll hear the kernels popping and hitting the sides and lid of the saucepan. It gets very noisy!

7. When the noise dies down to only a couple of pops a second, turn off the heat. Using an oven mitt, hold down the lid and shake the pan a few times to redistribute the kernels.

8. When the popping has stopped completely, take off the lid and empty your popcorn into a bowl.

Tip: One cup of unpopped kernels yields about six cups of popped corn.

GET SPRINKLING

Now you can add flavor to your basic popcorn. Choose one or more of these delicious toppings.

- For classic popcorn, add a little salt.

- For sweet popcorn, add sugar. Any type will do, though brown sugar is especially nice.

- Add a spoonful of honey or maple syrup and a handful of chopped nuts. (**Warning:** Don't add nuts if you are allergic to them.)

- Add a lump of butter and stir well.

- For spicy popcorn, try chili powder or cayenne pepper.

- Sift cocoa powder over the top and mix well.

- Sprinkle on finely grated Parmesan cheese.

HOW TO MAKE A SILHOUETTE PORTRAIT

People have made silhouette portraits of their friends and family for years. Expert artists can cut out an image freehand, but this simple technique works well, too.

You Will Need:

- a sheet of white paper
- sticky putty
- a lamp
- a pencil
- scissors
- glue
- a sheet of black paper

WHAT TO DO

1. Tack the sheet of white paper to a wall with some sticky putty.

2. Get your friend to sit in profile (sideways) next to the wall. Place a bright lamp beside him or her (make sure your friend is between the lamp and the paper). Move the lamp back and forth until your friend's shadow profile appears life-size on the white paper and not blurred.

3. Use the pencil to trace around the shadow on the paper.

4. Take the sheet of white paper down from the wall and cut out the silhouette along the pencil line you have made.

5. Glue the silhouette to a sheet of black paper to show it off best.

HOW TO PLAY CLOCK WATCHERS

All you need for this game is an alarm clock and three or more players. Make sure you cover up any other clocks in the room and confiscate all watches and cell phones!

Get everyone to stand in a circle. Set the alarm clock so that it will ring in about two minutes' time. The idea is for each player to sit down when he or she thinks the alarm is going to ring. Each player shouts out his or her name as he or she sits down. The last person to sit down before the alarm rings is the winner.

HOW TO TELL IF YOUR FRIEND IS A WEREWOLF

If you have a suspicion that on the night of a full moon your friend transforms herself into a wolflike creature, see the checklist below. If she matches more than five of the criteria, it's time to panic because she's definitely a werewolf!

- She's hopeless at karaoke — she howls rather than sings.
- She has red-tinged, curled fingernails.
- She gets restless whenever the moon becomes full.
- She never wears silver jewelry. Silver is a metal feared by werewolves, as they can be killed only by silver bullets.

- There are reported sightings of a strange creature roaming your street that always coincide with evenings your friend is not around at your house.

- Your goldfish tries to jump out of its bowl when your friend is in your bedroom. Your pet puppy whimpers, particularly when your friend tries to eat the food from its bowl when no one is looking.

- It is embarrassing to go out for a meal with your friend because she picks up her food with her hands, rips it apart with her teeth, and snarls at the waiter.

- Tell your friend that the first sign of being a werewolf is hairy palms. Then tell her that the second sign of being a werewolf is looking for hair on your palms. Watch to see if she turns over her hands to check them.

HOW TO MAKE FANCY "MOCKTAILS"

Invite a few friends over to enjoy some alcohol-free "mocktails." Find out how to create some delicious drinks and decorate the glasses.

THE RECIPES

Sea Breeze. Take a tall glass and add equal amounts of grapefruit juice and cranberry juice. Stir well and add plenty of crushed ice.

Green Monster. Squeeze the juice of a whole lime into a small glass. Top with lemonade and crushed ice. Add a slice of lime.

Cola Float. Pour some cola into a tall glass. Drop in two scoops of vanilla ice cream and stir.

Cinderella. Mix together equal amounts of pineapple juice, apple juice, and lemon juice. Pour into a tall glass and add a splash of sparkling lemonade.

THE DECORATION

Mocktails shouldn't just taste delicious. They should look good, too. Here are some ways to add some pizzazz to your drinks.

- Make colored ice cubes by adding food coloring to water before freezing it.

- Sugar-frost your glass before pouring in the drinks. Dip the rim in a little water, then in a saucer of sugar.

- Slices of fruit always look great. Make a small slit in a slice of orange and balance on the rim of the glass.

- Add a pretty straw — the twirlier the better.

- Add a paper umbrella.

HOW TO COLOR CARNATIONS

Give someone a bunch of flowers in his or her favorite color, even if it's blue, green, or black!

You Will Need:

- 1 1/4 cups water
- a clear jar
- 20 drops of food coloring in the color you want your flowers to be
- six white carnations

WHAT TO DO

1. Pour the water into the jar and add the food coloring.

2. Cut about 2 inches off the base of the stems of your carnations, then stand the flowers in the water.

3. Check every now and then, watching the flowers gradually change color over the next twenty-four hours. Even though they don't have roots, the stems of the flowers will suck up the colored water and transport it to the petals and leaves.

4. If your carnations don't start to show color in the petals within six hours, add some more food coloring to the water.

Tip: Red and blue food coloring work the best.

HOW TO BE A SYNCHRONIZED SWIMMER

If you're strong, flexible, and good at holding your breath underwater, synchronized swimming may be the perfect sport for you. It's all about performing routines in the water in complete harmony with the other swimmers on your team.

IMPRESS THE JUDGES

Here are ten steps to follow to become a champion synchronized swimmer.

1. Decide whether you're going to work as a pair or in a team. A maximum of eight girls can be in a team. Starting in a pair (known as a duet) is a good idea as it's easier to keep in time with one person than with a whole group.

2. Dress right. Make sure your team wears matching swimming suits and caps.

3. Put on a nose clip to keep the water from rushing up your nose when making upside-down underwater moves!

4. Choose your music carefully. Anything with a good beat is great, and songs from musicals are particularly good.

Warning: It is essential that you keep musical equipment away from the poolside.

5. Make a good impression on the judges before you even get in the pool by performing some fancy "deckwork." These are the movements done on the side of the pool before you enter

the water. But be quick! You're allowed only ten seconds of deckwork before you get in the pool.

6. Never touch the bottom of the pool with your hands or feet during the routine, as the judges will deduct points.

7. Practice keeping your eyes open underwater so you can see what your teammates are doing.

8. Practice holding your breath underwater. The best synchronized swimmers can stay under for up to a minute while performing complicated moves.

9. Practice the basic moves until they're second nature. Check out the mini guide on the opposite page.

10. Smile! Even if you're really exhausted, it's essential to smile to convince the judges and audience that what you're doing is easy.

THE ESSENTIAL MOVES

Here's a guide to the main moves in this sport.

Boost: A speedy headfirst rise out of the water, where you raise as much of your body as possible above the surface.

Cadence Action: A sequence of movements performed one-by-one by all team members, usually in rapid succession.

Twirl: A rapid twist of 180 degrees.

Ballet Leg: Each swimmer lies flat on the surface with one leg flat on the water and the other stretched straight up in the air.

Eggbeater: A leg kick that supports your whole body, leaving your arms free.

Vertical Position: This is when you position yourself upside down in the water, without touching the bottom. Your legs point straight up and out of the water.

HOW TO MAKE A DANCING PRINCESS GREETING CARD

Use the template on page 110 to make a beautiful and unique greeting card.

You Will Need:

- tracing paper
- a pencil
- some thin cardboard
- tape
- scissors
- four butterfly paper fasteners
- different-colored felt-tip pens
- large envelope

WHAT TO DO

1. Using the illustration on the opposite page, trace the princess's head, body, legs, and arms.

2. Place the tracing paper on top of the cardboard (use some tape to keep the tracing paper in place). Draw over the pencil lines again, pressing firmly so the pencil leaves an indented mark on the cardboard (draw the big dots where the holes will go, too).

3. Remove the tracing paper and go over the marks on the cardboard with the pencil, then cut out the cardboard shapes.

4. Pierce the big holes with the point of the scissors. Ask an adult for help with this!

5. Attach each of the legs and arms to the body of the princess with a butterfly paper fastener.

6. Color in the princess, drawing in her features, with felt-tip pens. Write a greeting on the back of the card. Put it in an envelope and send it to a friend.

HOW TO INTERPRET YOUR DREAMS

Experts say your dreams will give you clues about who you are and reveal your deepest emotions. Here are some of the most common dreams and what some people believe your inner self is trying to tell you when you dream them.

You're at School with No Clothes On. This may mean you feel exposed. Perhaps you've started at a new school or a new class and feel unprepared? Don't worry, you'll make friends and learn the ropes soon.

You're Flying. This dream could mean you're feeling creative, confident, and strong.

Your Teeth Fall Out. This common dream may mean you've been feeling very self-conscious about your appearance. Perhaps you've recently made some new friends and wonder what they think about you. Relax! The next time you see them, just smile and have a good time.

You're in a Beautiful Garden. This could mean you're feeling calm, happy, and stable.

You're Falling. This probably means you're feeling worried and insecure about something, such as finishing a project in time. Make sure you haven't taken on too much so you don't feel overwhelmed.

You See a Rainbow. This dream might reveal your hope for success in the future. A rainbow forms a bridge between what's happening today and what may happen tomorrow.

You've Lost Something Important. If you dream you have lost your house key or purse, it may mean you're worried about losing your position as best at something. Or maybe you've fallen out with a friend and need to make up.

You're Giving Money Away. This probably means you're a loving person.

You Dream About Your Teacher. You may be seeking advice, support, or guidance about something that's worrying you.

HOW TO MAKE POTPOURRI

Put together some potpourri, which is a mixture of dried flowers, herbs, spices, and citrus fruits. It not only looks pretty, but it will make your bedroom smell nice, too. Just remember that even though it might smell fruity and delicious, you can't eat potpourri. Here's what you can use:

FLOWERS

Any sweet-smelling flowers will do, though roses work really well. Get permission before you pick any flowers from the back-yard, or ask at the local florist for any discarded flowers and buds. Place the flower heads, buds, or petals in a warm, airy spot to dry out for a few days.

HERBS

Herbs with woody stems, such as lavender or rosemary, are the best to use as they're highly perfumed and dry well. Hang bunches to dry in an airy spot for around a week. Health-food stores are a good source of dried lavender, or you may be lucky enough to have some growing in your yard.

SPICES

Dried spices will really enhance the smell of your potpourri, and they look great, too. The best ones to try are cinnamon sticks, cloves, and star anise. Ask an adult if there are any out-of-date spices in the kitchen cupboard. The spices might not be good to cook with, but they're still fine to use for potpourri.

FRUIT

Dried fruit slices look pretty and have a wonderful scent. You can buy them ready-made or make them by slicing a citrus fruit thinly and drying the slices out in an oven at a low temperature for at least six to eight hours. A mixture of lemons, limes, and oranges looks really great.

Mix all your potpourri ingredients together.

Take your time arranging them in a pretty bowl. Any bowl will do, although wooden or glass bowls really emphasize the natural look of potpourri. Then place on a low table and enjoy!

ADDED EXTRAS

The wonderful thing about homemade potpourri is that you can keep adding to the mixture to change the way it looks and smells. For instance, you could include pretty pinecones, small seashells, miniature Christmas decorations, or pieces of bark.

Why not add a few drops of perfume oil after a while, when the natural scent of your potpourri starts to fade?

HOW TO MAKE YOUR OWN ICE POPS

Homemade ice pops are easy to make, especially if you get your hands on a plastic ice-pop mold. All you need to do is fill up the mold, put it in the freezer, and wait. If you don't have a special mold, use clean mini yogurt cups. Here are some great recipes.

BANANA AND HONEY

Mash up some banana. Mix it with milk and a delicious squirt of honey.

LOVELY LEMONADE

Add a squeeze of fresh lemon to some ordinary lemonade.

SMOOTHIE MOVE

Just pour in some of your favorite smoothie drink.

FRESH AND FRUITY

Simply mix equal quantities of fruit yogurt and fruit juice.

CHOCOLATE HEAVEN

Add chocolate syrup to milk.

Before your ice-pop mix is completely frozen, remove it from the freezer. Add a clean Popsicle stick to the middle of the mixture and return it to the freezer. That way you can hold your ice pop later when it's completely frozen.

Tip: Avoid pineapple, as anything with pineapple in it won't freeze.

HOW TO SLICE A BANANA WITHOUT PEELING IT

Give your friends a major surprise when they peel a banana and find that it is already miraculously cut into four pieces. They won't believe their eyes.

1. Thread a long needle with cotton thread. Starting at the tip of the banana, push the needle under the skin and wiggle it along the inside edge of the skin, as shown, until it comes out the other side.

2. Push the needle back through the same hole and keep wiggling. Repeat until you've slipped the thread right around the whole banana and brought the needle out through the original hole.

3. Remove the needle. Then hold both ends of the thread together and pull out – this will slice the banana inside the skin. Do this three times down the length of the banana. Put the banana in your lunch box and offer it to your friends at lunchtime.

HOW TO MAKE A FRIENDSHIP STONE

A friendship stone is a really special gift to give your best friend. He or she can proudly display it on a bedroom windowsill or use it as a paperweight on a desk.

You Will Need:

- a stone
- various colored paints
- paintbrushes
- colored felt-tip pens
- water-based acrylic varnish

WHAT YOU DO

1. Wash and dry the stone before you begin. Protect your work surface with newspapers and be sure the room is well ventilated.

2. Paint a design on the stone. You can choose any design you like. Adding your friend's initials is a nice touch. Let it dry.

3. Use the felt-tip pens (or paint) to write on the underside of the stone. This could be your friend's name or a message like "Best friends forever." Let it dry.

4. Paint on a coat of varnish to seal in your design and words.

5. Wait for the stone to dry completely, then give it to your friend.

Tip: You're not allowed to remove stones from certain beaches, so always check first. Garden centers sell bags of stones in various shapes and sizes. You may even find the perfect stone in the park or in your backyard.

HOW TO CATCH A SPIDER

If you'd rather not share your room with a spider, don't be tempted to squash it. Instead, you can capture it and transfer it elsewhere.

- If the spider is hanging out on a wall or windowsill, just place a clear glass over it. Slide a piece of stiff cardboard under the rim. You can now carry the spider safely out to the yard and release it.

- If the spider has spun a web, you'll need to hold the glass underneath, as spiders tend to drop down from their webs when they sense danger. Again, seal the spider inside the glass with a piece of cardboard.

- If a spider is crawling high up a wall or on a ceiling, try catching it on a feather duster. Once you've caught it, tip it into a glass and seal with cardboard.

HOW TO MAKE A SNOW GLOBE

Snow globes are easy to make and are beautiful gifts, although you'll probably want to keep one for yourself once you've made them. The great thing about snow globes is that you can put anything in them.

You Will Need:

- a lump of sticky putty
- a jar with a watertight screw-top lid (soak the jar in warm soapy water to peel off any label)
- small waterproof plastic toy or decoration
- water
- a bottle of glycerine (a syrupy liquid found in pharmacies and the baking aisle of supermarkets)
- a pitcher
- some glitter

WHAT DO DO

Here's how to make your own snow globe.

1. Stick a lump of sticky putty on the inside of the jar's lid. Mold the sticky putty into a hill shape, making sure you leave a gap around the edges so you'll be able to screw the lid back onto the jar later on.

2. Now it's time to create your snow globe scene. Stick a plastic toy into the top of the sticky putty. Make sure it will stay put even when held upside down or shaken. You can put anything you like inside your globe as long as it can be submerged in water.

3. Add equal parts of water and glycerine to a pitcher. Add a tablespoon of glitter to your mixture. This will be the snow in your globe. The glycerine will ensure that the glitter "snow" moves slowly in the water.

4. Pour your "snow" mixture into the jar.

5. Hold the jar over a sink in case of spills and twist on the lid. Be careful not to dislodge the figure from the sticky putty.

6. Turn the jar upside down, shake, and watch the snow swirl around your scene.

Tip: If you're making snow globes as gifts, tailor them to the occasion — add hearts for Valentine's Day, mini decorations for Christmas, and bunnies for Easter.

HOW TO
HOLLOW OUT AN EGG

If you want to decorate eggs and display them permanently as ornaments, you need to completely blow out the contents first — otherwise they'll start to smell. Here's how to do it:

1. First, ask an adult for help. Then wash and dry the egg gently.

2. Using a darning needle, very carefully puncture a tiny hole at the rounded end of the egg.

3. Now make a bigger hole at the pointed end of the egg. Push the needle right in to make sure you puncture the yolk.

4. Place the egg over a bowl and put your lips to the small hole, blowing until all the contents come out. Be careful not to suck in any of the raw egg. It can carry bacteria. However, you can use the contents to make an omelet or scrambled eggs when you're done.

5. Rinse the shell with cold running water and allow it to dry thoroughly before painting it. You can use paints, felt-tip pens, wax crayons, or food coloring to decorate your egg.

6. Finally, working in a well-ventilated room, paint on a coat of clear varnish to harden the egg and make sure it stays beautiful forever.

HOW TO PLAY FIVE STONES

Five Stones is an ancient game, played by children just like you for many centuries. All you need is five plastic or metal jacks (you can buy these in a toy store) or five stones each about the size of a penny.

WHAT TO DO

There are lots of different ways of playing Five Stones. This is a method that combines different skills.

To start, throw all five stones into the air with one hand and catch as many as you can on the back of the same hand.

Next, throw up all the stones that are on the back of your hand and try to catch them again in the palm of the same hand. If you end up with no stones in your hand and all of them on the ground, your turn is over.

If you managed to catch at least one stone, you can continue playing. Keep one of the stones in your hand and scatter all the others on the ground.

Throw the stone in your hand in the air and quickly pick up one of the stones from the ground. Catch the stone in the air before it falls to the ground. Do this for each of the stones on the ground.

Repeat this, but this time pick up two stones before catching the tossed stone. On the second throw, pick up the two remaining stones.

Repeat, picking up three stones and then one stone. Finally, pick up all four stones before catching the tossed stone.

The goal is to get through all the moves without dropping any stones.

When you are good enough at this, try adding in a clap or a knee slap before picking up stones.

HOW TO AMAZE YOURSELF

Here are two tricks to practice when you are alone. Once you know how to do them, perform them in front of your friends. They will all be convinced that you have magical powers.

LEVITATE YOUR ARM

Stand with both arms straight down by your sides. Move so you are standing next to a wall, with your right arm against it. Push the back of your right hand against the wall. Push hard while you count to thirty. Now quickly step away from the wall and turn so that your back is to the wall. Watch as your arm mysteriously floats upward.

LONG ARM, SHORT ARM

Now stretch your right arm out to the side of your body as far as you can reach. Move so that the tips of the fingers on your right hand are just touching the wall. Now bend your right arm, so the fingers touch your shoulder. With your other hand, rub your elbow. Then straighten your right arm again. You will find that it has mysteriously "shrunk" and your fingertips won't touch the wall. Weird!

IT'S NOT MAGIC

There's no magic involved in these two tricks. The movements of your bones, joints, and muscles are what make them work.

IF YOU LIKED THIS BOOK, BE SURE TO CHECK OUT:

The Girls' Book of Glamour: A Guide to Being a Goddess

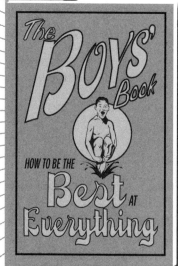
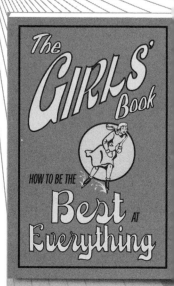

Treat your family to something AMAZING!

The **Family** Book

AMAZING THINGS TO DO TOGETHER

- OPTICAL ILLUSIONS AND MAGIC TRICKS
- MIND-BOGGLING PUZZLES AND RIDDLES
- UNIQUE ARTS AND CRAFTS

And more!